Denim Mending for Beginners

Patch and Repair Your Favorite Denim with Classic Japanese Stitching

© **Copyright 2019 - All rights reserved.**

The content contained within this book may not be reproduced, duplicated or transmitted without direct written permission from the author or the publisher.

Under no circumstances will any blame or legal responsibility be held against the publisher, or author, for any damages, reparation, or monetary loss due to the information contained within this book. Either directly or indirectly.

Legal Notice:

This book is copyright protected. This book is only for personal use. You cannot amend, distribute, sell, use, quote or paraphrase any part, or the content within this book, without the consent of the author or publisher.

Disclaimer Notice:

Please note the information contained within this document is for educational and entertainment purposes only. All effort has been executed to present accurate, up to date, and reliable, complete information. No warranties of any kind are declared or implied. Readers acknowledge that the author is not engaging in the rendering of legal, financial, medical or professional advice. The content within this book has been derived from various sources. Please consult a licensed professional before attempting any techniques outlined in this book.

By reading this document, the reader agrees that under no circumstances is the author responsible for any losses, direct or indirect, which are incurred as a result of the use of information contained within this document, including, but not limited to, — errors, omissions, or inaccuracies.

Table of Contents

Jikoshoukai: The Introduction 6

Chapter 1 - Tsuru: The Tools.......................... 10

Chapter 2 - Sashiko: The Little Stabs 14

Chapter 3 - Kantha: The Patched Cloth 26

Chapter 4 - Boro: The Repaired 38

Chapter 5 - Patchi: The Patch 50

Chapter 6 - Yoeki: The Solution..................... 62

Leave A Review? 76

Ketsuron: The Conclusion.............................. 78

Jikoshoukai: The Introduction

People have been sewing for a very long time.

20,000 years ago, during the Ice Age, someone decided that punching a hole through needles and running threads through them seemed like a good way to sew.

They were right.

Archeologists have uncovered needles made of bone and concluded that early humans used them to sew furs and skins. But bone needles required, well, bones. There had to be a better material to utilize.

Fast forward to the year circa 100 B.C. Parts of Northern Europe began to use iron needles. These were sturdier than any previous forms of needles used (bronze was used to make needles around 3,000 B.C., and these had been in use until iron replaced them).

Today, you have sewing needles made from materials such as carbon steel (for that extra durability) and 18K gold (for corrosion resistance and for those who do not mind splurging a little on tools).

It is not just the tools of sewing that have evolved over the years. Even the reason behind the art of sewing has shifted perspective. At one point in time, it was a craft used for necessity. People could not afford to risk sacrificing animals they used as food to mend a torn shirt. These days, sewing has turned into a hobby. It has become a way for people to enjoy an art that requires a considerable amount of skill. It has even become a way to improve your mood and help you relax.

Even technology has helped add convenience and sophistication to the art. Thomas Saint is known as the designer of the first sewing machine. Although, a German by the name of Charles Weisenthal had issued a patent for a machine that used needle nearly 30 years before Thomas Saint's design. Because of this reason, there has been some debate on the matter of the actual inventor of the sewing machine.

Regardless of the machine's origins, people and industries both use the machine today to create and repair garments, fabrics, clothing, and fashion products.

Companies use workshops that contain sewing machines to manufacture textiles, and those textiles are used to create clothing and apparel.

In many cases, manufacturers produce the article of clothing themselves, especially if the manufacturer is a home-based business. From tops and trousers to dresses of all kinds, sewing comes into play in the creation of many clothing products, and in the mending of those products as well.

Need a solution to fix a tear? Why, sew the tear together. Is there a way to make some modifications to a garment? No problem, bring out the needle and thread.

This capability to sew damaged clothing allows clothes to last for a long time. It makes them reusable. It helps maintain them.

It makes them sustainable, even in the world of fashion.

Chapter 1 - Tsuru: The Tools

Tools of the Trade

Even though a sewing machine speeds up the mending process, hand sewing is often preferred. This is because sewing performed by hand allows you to take the time to create wonderful and high quality handcrafted results. In many cases, the results speak for themselves, as you get to see the work of a person who applied finesse and patience to create a spectacular finish.

This is what you will be producing: works of incredible quality that showcase your skills.

When people think about the tools that are required for sewing, they often imagine the needle, thread, and scissors. While those are definitely the essentials, each sewing process requires a different set of tools. Take, for example, the process of marking the cloth. You have markers to show you where the pleat should fall on the garment, where the dart should be inserted, and so much more. Looking through the different markers, you have so many options such as water-soluble ink pens, the ever popular tailor's chalk, the tracing wheel, and a lot more. Those are just for the markers.

You have tools for ripping seams. You have special tools for opening buttonholes.

For the work that we shall be doing, we will dispense with the tools that are clearly meant for veterans of the art. We are not working with seams and buttons, so we won't require any tools that attend to those parts.

What we have left are tools that are important for you. These are the basic tools that will help you perfect some of the techniques that we are going to focus on.

Before you can start working on your material, you need to organize your tools. It is always preferable to keep all essential tools near you so that you are prepared before you begin mending. One of the reasons for this is that while you are mending, you often lose yourself in the work. Sewing requires a fair degree of concentration, and you might not want to be distracted while you are engrossed in a particular stitch.

Here are the tools you may require:

- A sharp needle. Ensure that you are not using worn or damaged needles, as they might cause damage to the denim while stitching. For specific stitches or threads, make sure that you get the right needle. To highlight an example, sashiko thread goes perfectly with sashiko needles.

- Thread. The choice of thread is important because when you use a thread that does not match your requirements, it only creates a poor result. There are a lot of factors to consider such as elasticity of the thread, its seam strength, its chemical resistance, and more. So ideally, you should get a high-quality thread and the right one for specific stitches.

- Pins. For holding the cloth in pace. After all, you only have two hands.

- An iron to smooth out the fabric. This allows you to work on the denim more easily. Additionally, with an iron, you can remove any folds or creases that might hinder your work process.

When you are ready, let us dive in to the first stitch.

Chapter 2 - Sashiko: The Little Stabs

Sashiko is a form of classic Japanese embroidery that makes use of curved or straight linear patterns to form stitches. In other words, it uses curved or straight stitches made in a repeating pattern. The name itself means "little pierce" or "little stabs." The name is used to describe its technique, that of a running stitch that has numerous little stitches.

What makes Sashiko special is the fact that no one knows of the technique's exact origins. All they know is that it developed in rural areas in Northern Japan. From there, it spread along the trade routes to different parts of the world.

The spread of the technique occurred during the Edo period as early as 1615, which is why by the time the Meiji period arrived in 1868 the technique was already well established in various parts of Japan.

Sashiko stitches are usually sewn into fabrics and materials using a white thread on an indigo background or fabric. This was because most Japanese families were too poor to afford dyes and colorings. They utilized whatever materials they could get their hands on, and blue fabric was one of the most common materials available during that era.

Today, sashiko patterns are a beautiful addition to a wardrobe. They are versatile in that you can apply them on almost any piece of material. As they are hand-sewn, you can adapt the technique to fit different patterns for various articles of clothing.

We are going to utilize this technique to create stitches that are not only effective in mending your denim, but add a simple design that creates a wonderful effect. Whenever you are ready, let us find out just what materials you might require for the process.

Materials Required

You will need all the materials mentioned in Chapter 1. Do make sure that you are using sashiko needles and threads for this stitching. You will also require the below equipment:

- Scissors

- Fabric chalk for markings. **PRO TIP:** If you do not have fabric chalk, you can also make use of dry soap (wet soap is, of course, slippery and does not make for a fun sewing experience).

- Ruler
- The right fabric (discussed below)

The Right Fabric

Traditionally, people use Sashiko on dye-fabrics, particularly indigo dye. But that is not a rule set in stone. Any color of fabric will do, provided that the fabric is smooth and even.

PRO TIP: when choosing the size of the fabric, make sure that it not only covers the gap or hole you are about to mend, but extends beyond the hole's borders to cover a large area. In other words, choose a fabric that is almost the same size as the hole. However, in many cases, people have been known to use the exact measurements as the gap that they would like to stitch. This has its own advantages that we shall discuss further below. As you are getting started, we are going to give you enough surface area to work with.

For example, if the hole you are mending is 3 inches by 2 inches, then you should ideally choose a fabric that is 5 inches by 5 inches.

This allows you to have an extra area around the hole to extend your pattern. The amount of area you would like to work with depends on your preference. You can use a bigger fabric so that you can add a bigger pattern to your denim.

Pattern

For our stitch, we shall go ahead and use a classic sashiko pattern. This is a simple pattern that allows you to complete the work quickly and also acts as a primer to get you started on sashiko stitches. Mastering it is relatively easy and once you get used to it, you can move on to more complex patterns. The basic idea that we are going to employ is that you keep the stitches going until you complete the pattern.

Our first step is to use a chalk or any other form of marker to draw the lines on which we shall be performing the stitch. This applies not just for this instance, but to all stitches that you might work on in the future.

The pattern we will be using for this stich is a lined pattern. We will be working with multiple parallel lines. You will understand how to create the lines in the following section, but for now, it is important to know the basic idea of the stitch.

The number of lines you require depends on the size of the gap on the fabric. Let us assume that you have a gap that is three inches wide. You are ideally looking to add around six to seven lines that run across the gap.

I would recommend adding the lines lengthwise along the denim. This makes the stitch easier to work with for beginners. However, you could work with diagonal lines (based on the position of the fabric).

Each line features a quarter of an inch stitch, followed by an equally long gap, then a quarter long stitch, a gap, and so on until you have mended the patch.

It is not necessary for each stitch to be parallel to the others, as long as the lines along which the stitches are made are parallel.

Getting to Work

Now that you have your pattern ready, it is time to perform the stitch.

Step 1:

The first thing that you should do is ensure that the gap or hole is devoid of any stray threads.

I use the term "stray threads" to talk about those threads that surround the hole and are usually uneven.

Take your scissors and cut off these threads.

You do not have to make each cut perfect. You are merely removing those strands of thread that are jutting out too much.

Step 2:

You are now going to use your chosen fabric to cover the area.

Place the fabric on the inner side of the denim. This is the side that comes into contact with your body, with the side that is visible being the outer side of the denim. Make sure the hole is covered properly.

When you are satisfied with the result, use your pins to secure the fabric.

Step 3:

Take out your fabric chalk (or your dry soap), and start making lines on the outer side of the denim. Use your ruler to make the lines straight.

PRO TIP: Once you have made your first line, take a step back to see if you have aligned the ruler properly for the next line. What you should also do is make sure that your lines match the area of the fabric placed below the hole.

There is no point in adding a line on a part of the denim that does not have fabric underneath. Additionally, your first line should start close to the edge of the fabric in order to allow for as many lines as possible.

The gap between each line can be either half an inch or a quarter of an inch. However, the smaller the gap between the lines, the more thread you might require to finish the job.

Step 4:

Take out your Sashiko needle and thread it with about 19 – 25 inches of sashiko thread. Try to keep the length between the aforementioned measurements or else you will have a thread that dangles a lot. This makes for an uncomfortable sewing experience.

Step 5:

Add a knot to one end of the thread. Choose the line that is closer to the edge of the patch. Now take your needle and insert it from the bottom of the patch (from the inner side of the denim).

Additionally, make sure that you are starting at the top or bottom of the line, and not somewhere in between.

What you are about to do is use a technique called "running stitch." In this technique, you will make sure that you are not going to pull the thread through after you have inserted the needle.

This means that the stitches you add to the fabric will be continuous as you move from one stitch to the other.

Step 6:

Now you are going to start creating the stitches. Each stitch should be around a quarter of an inch long.

Here is a great way to keep track of your stitches. Starting from the inner side, pierce the denim. Measure quarter inches, and then pierce again.

Then measure quarter inches again and pierce the denim again. Continue doing this. Make sure you do not pull the thread through or you will have a difficult time getting back on track.

When you reach the end of the line, ensure that the needle is on the inner side of the denim before moving on to the other line.

When you reach the other line, pierce through the denim and bring back the needle to the outer side. Measure ¼ inches and pierce through and continue repeating the pattern you created on line one.

PRO TIP:

Do not worry if the stitches are not uniform. You are just starting out. The most important thing for you to do is enjoy the process. Immerse yourself into the technique and get into the flow of things. There is no need to be perfect. As you keep practicing the technique, you will gain mastery over it.

Uneven stitches are also designs of their own, in many ways. See if you can use that to your advantage and make a unique pattern out of it.

Step 7:

If you find yourself running out of thread, then make a knot on the inner side of the denim and tie it off.

PRO TIP: Anticipate the fact that you are running out of thread and make sure that you reach the end of a line before you create the knot, rather than having the thread run out in the middle of a line. It is much easier to start from the top or bottom of the line than from the middle.

Step 8:

Continue creating the stitches until you have

covered all the lines you have made.

PRO TIP: Take a pause occasionally to smooth out the denim. This removes any unevenness and helps you create better stitches. You can use an iron if you like, but do not take too much time using the iron. Just a quick swipe to smooth out the denim should do.

Step 9:

When you have finished with the last line, create a knot (any simple knot will suffice) on the inner side and complete your stitch.

Step 10:

Admire your handiwork!

As you can see, by using a simple pattern, you have turned a piece of denim that had a flaw into a work of art. You are now the envy of your friends!

PRO TIP:

- There is a reason why we use sashiko thread for this process. The thread is thicker and most importantly, it is twisted in a unique way. Even if you have a thread that has the same thickness as sashiko, do not replace the sashiko thread with it.

- Some people have known to sharpen their needle before using it. This is not necessary. In fact, sharpening the needle might end up dulling it if done improperly. However, I do recommend that you know how to sharpen your needles so that when you do spot signs of dullness, you are prepared for it. In the beginning, what you should think of doing is getting yourself a high quality needle. Manufacturers already keep the needle sharp and ready for the sewing process.

- If you feel that the needle tends to apply pressure on your finger and leaves behind blisters, then you could avoid the discomfort by getting a thimble. A thimble is simply a small plastic or metal cap worn on your finger in order to protect it. You typically place it on the finger that you use to push the needle. Let us take an example. If you tend to push the needle using your middle finger, then go ahead and place your thimble on it. If you notice yourself pushing the needle with your forefinger, then that is where you need to place your thimble.

Chapter 3 - Kantha: The Patched Cloth

A famous method of marketing certain fabrics and cloth in India involves prefixing them with the word "Kantha." You will often find names such as "Kantha blankets," "Kantha fabrics," and so on. The word itself is a selling point because it denotes a type of craft that deals with precision and quality. The word "kantha" has two meanings:

- In one meaning, the word translates to "patched cloth." This meaning refers to kantha's ability to patch together various fabrics to create unique quilts.

- Another meaning refers to the type of stitch used on fabrics.

However, kantha mainly refers to the type of stitching that is commonly found in Bangladesh, or in the Indian state of West Bengal.

When you look through history, you can trace back this style of embroidery all the way back to the pre-Vedic ages. Like many forms of embroidery, kantha utilizes motifs to a greater degree. A majority of these motifs are representations of nature. They focus on elements such as the sun, the universe, and on many occasions, the tree of life. To people using the kantha stitching form, it was merely a way of life. They used it to sew together torn garments or fabrics. It wasn't a marketable skill, and they were definitely not focused on creating customers for it.

That soon changed. Kantha began to spread to various parts of the world. This spread occurred mainly because of the use of kantha in Hindu festivals, traditions, and occasions. From weddings to social occasions to religious events, kantha began to be viewed by more and more people. Soon, there were people who wanted to know more about it. They wanted to try out the stitchings themselves. They wanted to practice it.

Some of them wanted to create products made out of kantha stitches.

What makes this embroidery special is that for centuries, Indian women have been using old cloths or discarded materials and stitching them together using a running stitch. They have transformed materials that were old and useless into something beautiful and useful. In fact, the entire idea behind kantha was to create something to provide warmth and protection, which is why it resulted in the creation of exquisite blankets based on centuries of experience. Eventually, the method of stitching took on a life of its own. It shifted from merely stitching blankets to mending various fabrics and garments.

Materials Required

You will need all the materials mentioned in Chapter 1. For the kantha method, you do not need a specific type of needle. My only recommendation is that you use high-quality needles that are not bent or worn out. Apart from the materials mentioned in Chapter 1, do note the materials below:

- Scissors
- Fabric chalk for markings. If you do not have fabric chalk, you can also make use of dry soap.
- Ruler
- The right fabric (discussed below.)

Fabric for Kantha

When it comes to Kantha, you can work with

any fabric. But as you are mending denim, I would recommend getting a similar denim fabric as the one used by your article of clothing.

PRO TIP: Should you feel like you want to, consider getting a fabric that is a shade lighter or a shade darker than your denim clothing. This makes for an interesting effect and allows you to add a sense of uniqueness into your clothing.

Additionally, having a darker shade can help you blend the fabric in with the denim fairly well. It won't entirely disappear, but it won't be noticeable, either.

Pattern

The best part about Kantha is that it incorporates numerous stitching techniques to create wonderful patterns. Not only do you get to work with different patterns, but you can also see the technique used for creating incredible patterns on items such as tote bags, belts, quilts, jackets, and other accessories. But we shall, of course, be working on denim, and to get you started on the technique, we are going to utilize one of its simple patterns.

This time, we are going to use a spiral pattern to create our designs.

With the spiral design, you automatically get used to working with curves. This, when combined with the lines that we practiced with in the sashiko technique, will allow you to create spectacular ideas for your stitching patterns.

So let us get started.

The first step you have to take is to make sure that you have placed your fabric right. We are going to use the same method to place fabric as we did in the sashiko technique. We will place it on the inner side of the denim (the side that comes into contact with your body). Remember that the fabric should be larger than the hole (for now, until you are used to the stitching technique).

When the fabric is large, you will notice that when placing the fabric, you not only cover the hole, but you also ensure that you work with stitches around the hole.

When you have arranged the fabric underneath the hole, the next step is to draw the pattern. Here are a few tips that you can follow to make sure you get the pattern right.

- The starting point of your pattern should be near the edge of the fabric. However, you can choose any edge if you like. For example, if your fabric is shaped like a square, you now have four edges. Your spiral pattern can commence near any edge.

- Take your time when drawing the spiral. You need it to go inwards towards the center of your design.

- As you draw the spiral, you will start to notice that there are numerous concentric circles. The space between each circle should ideally be the same.

- However, you can intentionally create the spiral with a few flaws in its shape, just to give it a unique twist. Do make sure that none of the lines intersect each other.

Once you have completed the job, take a step back to examine the result. Make sure that you are satisfied with how the design looks.

If you think that you might have to change the shape, do it now before you begin stitching.

Because you will be working with a slightly more complicated stitching technique, you might require a little more practice to get it done perfectly. For this reason, take your time stitching the pattern. Enjoy the process itself.

If you feel that you have made a mistake, then you have nothing to worry about. That is what scissors are for. Simply snip away the threads that have gone, let's say "off-track," and continue on with your work.

When you are ready to continue, let us begin to stitch the design into the denim.

Getting to Work

Step 1:

Ideally, you should start at one end of the spiral. You could begin at the end that lies in the center of the spiral design or the one that lies near the edge of the fabric (as discussed above.)

I would ideally recommend stitching based on how you created the spiral. As you started drawing the spiral from the edge of the fabric and moved to the center, you could begin your stitch from that point and slowly move towards the center as well.

The main reason for this is that we will be stitching back in the opposite direction. So it is better to get used to going in one direction first.

Step 2:

As with the sashiko technique, choose anywhere from 19 inches to 25 inches of thread. If we require more, then we can knot off the thread the way we did in the Sashiko technique and then add more thread.

Step 3:

Start from the inner side and pierce through the fabric to bring the needle to the outer side. We will now begin to follow the rules of the running stitch method. Add a quarter of an inch stitch and then pierce through. Let there be a gap of about a quarter of an inch, and then create another quarter inch stitch. Continue doing this as you work your way around the spiral towards the center.

Step 4:

If you run out of thread, then you can create a knot on the inner side of the denim and tie it off. As we are not working with straight lines, it is not easy to guess exactly how much thread we might require before we reach the end.

Once you have created the knot, add a new thread. Measure about a quarter of an inch and then continue with your stitch. Begin on the inner side of the denim. Pierce through, measure a quarter of an inch, and then go back to creating your running stitch pattern.

Continue doing this as you move towards the center of the spiral.

Depending on the size of the spiral, you could be using multiple threads to get the job done. Once you reach the middle, make sure you end the stitch on the inner side of your denim. Use a knot to finish the first part of your stitch.

Once you are done, we can now move on to the next phase of the stitch.

Step 5:

We will now be moving backwards along the spiral. For the first phase, you moved from the outer side of the spiral towards the center. This time, we are going to start at the center and back our way towards the starting point of our stitch.

What you are going to do now is cover up all the gaps that were created during your initial run of the stitch. As we are starting at the center of the spiral, find the final gap of your stitch (this should be the gap that is closest to the center of the spiral).

Step 6:

As always, we are going to start on the inner side of the denim. Pierce through and create your first stitch in such a way that it covers the gap.

Once the stitch is complete, your needle should be back on the inner side of the denim.

PRO TIP: If possible, do not cut off the thread after you had completed the first phase of the stitch. Without cutting, bring the thread back around to fill up the first gap. This creates a better result for you once you have completed the entire stitch.

Step 7:

Continue stitching all the way back to the starting point. If you run out of thread at any point, simply create a knot on the inner side of the denim and use a fresh thread to continue your stitch.

Eventually, you will have all the gaps stitched as well.

The result is that you now have a spiral that does not have a single gap in it. The best part about this technique is that if you look at the inner side of the denim, you will notice that there are no gaps there, either.

PRO TIP:

- After you have completed drawing the spiral design on the denim, you could place the thread on the design to find out approximately just how much thread you might require in the end for the stitch. When you have discovered the length of the thread, simply add another three or four inches to it. This extra length becomes useful when you have reached the end of the spiral and plan to continue backwards.

- If you do not mind working with a long thread, then simply use the above measurements and double the length of the thread you would like to use. This should give you enough thread to work your way towards one direction and then back again.

- Variety is spice, after all! So try choosing a color that compliments your denim's color. For example, if it is blue (which it typically is), then you could use tones that have low contrast like grey, purple, or even black. However, should you wish to add a dash of bright and warm colors, then choose to use high contrast shades such as red, orange, or yellow.

- The best way to work with colors is by placing them against the denim. Try each color and examine it from afar. See how the color looks on your denim. More importantly, ensure that you are comfortable with the color combination. If you feel that none of the colors mentioned above work for you, then try out a different color of your choice and then check out the effect it has on your denim. Whatever shade you choose, let it add a bit of personality in your stitch and bring out an incredible finish.

- A way to keep track of whether you are doing the technique right or wrong is by looking at both sides of the denim. You should be able to notice the gap-stitch-gap pattern on both sides. After you have completed the kantha stitch, you should notice no gaps on either side of the denim.

Chapter 4 - Boro: The Repaired

Boro has gained somewhat of a reemergence in recent times because of the way in which manufacturers and brands can utilize it to create stylish and chic clothing. What makes boro unique is its ability to utilize different fabrics to get a desired result.

Unlike other forms of stitching, the rise of boro was due to a sense of necessity. Its use was accepted more to accommodate the mending of torn and damaged fabrics than to create any sense of aesthetic presentation.

This style of stitching was popular in the rural areas of Japan during the eighteenth and nineteenth century. This was because cotton was not introduced into Japanese culture until well into the twentieth century. When a particular piece of clothing or covering material began to show signs of gaps or thinning, the family who owned the materials would find any piece of fabric that they could find. They would utilize the technique of sashiko stitching to get the job done.

Since rural families could not afford to purchase

new articles of clothing, they would continue to use the damaged garment for as long as possible, often handing them over to the next generation. These garments would continue to gain more patches as they suffered more holes and tears. Eventually, what was left was a garment that was devoid of its original design (or even colors).

When these fabrics that had received boro stitching were discovered during World War 2, it created a renewed interest in the method. What was once a technique utilized for living in moderate comfort soon became a fashion sense that spread to different parts of the world. However, to many Japanese, the boro fabrics were a remnant of a past that reminded them of their rural upbringings.

But as the adage goes, time does heal all wounds.

In modern day Japan, people have begun to adopt boro stitching as a way to work with fabrics. There are companies that especially work with the boro technique to create fashionable garments and accessories.

We are going to use this incredible technique to mend denim. We will see how boro stitching can create such a wonderful splash of color, fun, and style out of your torn garments.

Let us begin.

Materials Required

You will need all the materials mentioned in Chapter 1. For the boro method, it would be ideal to use the sashiko needle. You should also use sashiko thread to work with boro stitches. As always, I recommend using high-quality needles that are not bent or worn out. Apart from the materials mentioned in Chapter 1, do note the materials below:

- Scissors

- Fabric chalk for markings. If you do not have fabric chalk, you can also make use of dry soap.

- Ruler

- The right fabric (discussed below).

Fabric

When you are working with the boro technique, you have a choice between two fabric palettes:

- You can choose to stick to indigo dyes and find various shades of indigo, blues, and other similar hues.

- You can add in a dash of other complimentary neutral shades such as blacks, browns, and whites to bring a pop of color.

- One of the things that we are going to try is using different fabrics for the same patch. You could also use one single fabric to get the desired result. However, to add more personality to your denim, you could try multiple fabrics.

- A good way to decide if you are indeed looking for a single fabric or numerous colors to cover up the gap in your denim is to place your choice of cloth against the denim. Place them the way you would like the finished stitch to appear. Then see if you are satisfied with the result.

I would also recommend getting plainly woven, light fabrics that do not have tight stitches.

So whenever you are ready, let us move on to creating a pattern.

Pattern

We are going to be working with a running stitch again. This is because boro uses the techniques of sashiko to complete the mend. However, this time, we are going to work along the borders of the fabric. So if your fabric should look like a piece of square or a rectangle, your stitches will have a square or rectangular finish.

The arrangement of the fabric depends on the number of fabrics you have chosen for the stitch. But regardless of how many materials you have chosen, we will still be working along the border. Confused? Don't worry. It will become clear as we work our way with the stitches.

Getting to Work

Step 1:

Place the fabric on the inner side of your denim the way you want to stitch it. If you are using multiple fabrics, place them beside each other. Make sure that a part of one fabric overlaps the other so that they can be stitched together.

Let us assume that you have three fabrics now; blue, black, and white. Place the blue fabric first. Then place the black fabric on beside it, but let a small part of it fall over the blue fabric. In a similar manner, use the white fabric in such a way that a part of its edges falls on the black fabric.

If you would like to avoid arranging the fabrics in the manner described above, then you have an alternative. Try the below technique.

Take out your trusty scissors and create strips of fabrics.

Now examine the hole that you would like to mend. If the gap is mostly a horizontal tear, then place your strips of fabric vertically to allow each of them to appear through the gap. In a similar manner, if the tear is mostly vertical, then place the strips horizontally. Ensure that the strips overlap each other slightly so that you will be able to stitch them together. The size of each strip depends on the size of the tear. Let us say that the tear is 5 inches wide and 2 inches tall. Each of your strips should be 2 inches wide and roughly four inches tall. This allows you to arrange the strips in a manner where each strip can be noticed and also ensures that the hole is covered properly. Once you are done, secure the fabrics with pins.

If you are using just a single fabric, then you don't have to worry about adjusting it. Taking the above example of a tear which is 5 inches wide and 2 inches tall, simply find yourself a bit of fabric that is 6 inches wide and 4 inches tall. With that, you are good to go.

Once you have your fabrics ready, make sure that you pin them together.

Step 2:

Now that you have put your fabric or fabrics together, it's time to create your markings. For each side of the arrangement, draw two parallel lines. This means that you should typically have four pairs of lines if your fabric is square or rectangularly shaped.

It does not matter if your lines end up intersecting each other. You can use the intersections to make your pattern look unique.

Step 3:

Next, take out your sashiko needle and thread it with your sashiko thread. If you like, you can use a comfortable thread length of 19 to 24 inches. However, you can also place the thread against your markings and then check for the exact length that you will require for the stitch.

You can now perform the stitch in two ways. You can start with one line and begin sewing it constantly until you reach back to where you started from, or you can start with one straight line, stitch it, and then knot it before moving on to another line. I personally prefer the first option, as it is smoother and takes less time.

Step 4:

As always, start from the inner side of the denim and then begin your stitches. Use the running stitch method and keep your stitches and gaps at a quarter of an inch.

Step 5:

Make sure that when you reach a corner, you move your stitch to the next side and continue stitching.

Remember this. Since you have a pair of lines, you will have the outer shape and the inner shape.

What does this mean?

Let us look at it with an example.

Let us say that your fabric is square shaped. The lines that you draw on your fabric will also be shaped as a square. Because you are going to use parallel lines, it will look like you have a square that contains another small square within it.

Which is why - when you start stitching – you should make sure that you are focusing on the outer shape first.

Only after you have completed stitching the outer shape should you move on to the inner shape.

Step 6:

Make sure that you have completely stitched the outer shape and created a knot. Once that is done, proceed to stitching the inner shape.

Step 7:

Once again, use the running stitch method to create the stitches for the inner shape. You might use a shorter thread length to complete this section since the shape itself is smaller.

Step 8:

You can stop any time in the process to iron out creases or folds. This will allow you to work with a smoother surface. Furthermore, uneven surfaces prevent you from making accurate measurements. The result is an awkward finish where you have certain stitches meeting the length criteria of a quarter of an inch and others looking longer.

Step 9:

When you are done, take a step back to admire

your work.

PRO TIP:

- One of the things that you can do is practice the stitch on a sashiko kit. These incredible practice tools allow you to hone your craft before you can actually put them into practice.

    o These kits come with surfaces that have marked lines. Stitch along these marked lines until you are comfortable working those stitches on fabric.

- Muscle memory is a fantastic ability of the human body. It is why guitarists are able to perfect their skills and artists can draw their ideas without much effort. In the same way, the more practice you perform, the more your muscle memory improves.

    o Using the sashiko kits mentioned above, make sure that you try out different stitches. I would recommend starting with the running stitch, which you can use on practically any garment and for several purposes. Once you have perfected that, move on to other forms of stitches that provide a bit more challenge to you.

- You are only limited by your creativity. Seek out ways to add color to your garments wherever you see fit.

- If you find yourself unable to find fabrics, then you could use old clothes in your house. The best part about using old clothes is that you do not have to discard what remains. You can simply use it for another garment that requires stitching.

- Try to create your own designs and find ways to implement them. This process might allow you to flex your creativity and discover your own style for doing things.

- Here is an important point to remember: there is no such thing as a mistake in stitching. You are beginning your stitching journey and the most important factor is that you are having fun.

- If you find yourself in a situation where

the thread might seem too thick, then you could try separating the strands to make a thinner thread.

- Your garment will be divided into two segments: the stitched areas and the stitch-free areas. Whenever you are adding stitches, think about how the stitch-free areas might look. This way, you can actually create interesting designs and patterns.

Chapter 5 - Patchi: The Patch

There are many ways one can use a patch.

Getting a hole or a tear in clothing is inevitable. But, there are many ways to repair the damage caused. This is where patches become important. All you have to do is pick out the damaged garment and then mend its tears by using a patch above it.

You could add a patch as an addition to your clothing, giving it a sense of style or adding a unique perspective to an old material.

Additionally, some clothing – like uniforms – come with patches on them or require patches. You could hand sew these patches.

Or, you could add a pocket to a shirt. The idea is the same. You simply have to sew the preferred patch into the shirt, right where you would like the pocket to be. However, the only difference this time is that you have to keep one side open (which, of course, is the top of the pocket).

In many ways, patches are fun to work with because you can create incredible designs with them. You can use a multitude of shapes and colors to come up with your own spectacular results.

We have already seen many ways to sew an underhand patch, which is a patch that lies underneath the garment or, as per the phrase used in this book, the inner side of the garment (the side that comes into contact with your skin).

Now, we shall take a look at how we can create an overhand patch. This patch falls outside the garment. In other words, you sew it into the face of the garment.

Before you begin to sew the patch, you must get your garment ready for the process. There are a couple of steps that you can follow to make this happen. Here is how you can make that happen:

Step 1:

Make sure that you wash and dry the item of clothing on which you would like to stitch a patch. This is especially true for new articles of clothing. If you patch them up and then decide to wash them, you might notice that the material underneath the fabric will bunch up. This would make it necessary to remove the patch and try to sew a new one in its place, which I am guessing you wouldn't want to do.

Additionally, if you are using cotton, the fabric tends to shrink after you wash it for the first time. If you stitch the fabric before you run your clothing through the wash, then the material under the patch might shrink, causing the patch to shrink and bunch up as well.

Step 2:

The next step that you should take is to iron your clothing before you apply a patch to it. This helps you to avoid working on creases, which not only give you an uneven surface to work with that puts your measurements off, but also bunches up your patch.

The most important point to remember is that you should ensure that you iron out the area where you are going to apply the patch properly. If you can do that, then you may not have to use the iron again when you are adding your patch.

Choosing the Fabric

If you take a look at the market, there is no shortage of fabrics that you can use for your patchwork. However, one of the most important questions that one has to ask is what kind of fabric should one use?

You might think that simply picking an option that has the right color might just suit your purposes. However, that is far from the truth.

So which fabric should you use? Well, there are a few options that you can work with. I recommend using natural fabrics that have a tight weave. Let us take a look at some of the natural fabrics in the market such as cotton, wool, linen, and silk. Not only do they have the right weave, but they are also the best fabrics to use for hand sewing. Their surfaces are strong and you can easily create decorative stitching on them. One of the best features of the aforementioned natural fabrics is that you can pass your needles through them smoothly. This is because they include fibers that are woven in a cross pattern, creating minute gaps for you to use.

Let us now explore each of the above fabrics and understand why they are ideal for sewing. Once we cover their properties, I will let you know which fabric works the best for denim.

Cotton

Probably the most commonly used fabric is cotton. However, you might find quite a few varieties of cotton on the market. The trick is to pick out the right one. Thankfully, you have yours truly to guide you. You should be looking to get yourself a quilting cotton. The main reason for this choice is that quilting cotton is made to fit sewing and embroidery purposes. Plus, it is easily available on the market because of its use.

Linen

This material is lighter than cotton, but it is also slightly stronger. Linen is made using raw materials from the flax plant, and many even consider it as the strongest form of natural fibers. You can use this material to add a bit of durability to your finish. Linen is also a good conductor of heat. This means that it can sap away the body heat from you easily, keeping you much cooler than other fabrics.

Silk

Here is a common misconception about silk; people often think that the material can tear easily. But the reality is far different. In fact, it is a well-known fabric because of its tensile strength, which allows it to withstand strong pulls. Another feature of silk that makes it preferred my many embroiderers is the fact that it is also slightly elastic. This makes silk easy to work with and provides ease-of-use when sewing. Furthermore, silk does not wrinkle easily, retaining its original shape as much as possible.

Wool

Wool is a rather resilient fabric. It can not only handle heat well, but it is not affected by mold and mildew (two forms of fungus). Wool also prevents allergies by keeping dust mites away from your skin. In fact, dust mites do not like wool at all! The fabric can also keep you cool during summer. In short, wool is a strong and incredible fabric to work with for patches.

Fabric Mistakes

One of the most common mistakes that people make when choosing a fabric is that they look at the aesthetics and the colors more than the material itself. It can be easy to fall prey to this situation. After all, when you look at a fabric that has a certain appeal, you obviously imagine the many ways in which you can use that fabric.

What you should be doing instead is finding the right fabric for the project you are working on. Let us take a look at denim. You would never try to add silk to the material, as they do not go well together. However, silk does provide an assortment of colors that you can work with, making it a rather tempting fabric to you.

The best fabric that you can use for denim is

regular cotton. You can choose to use quilted cotton as well, but using regular cotton is easier since you more than likely have materials at home that you can use.

Now that you have an idea of the fabric to use, here is how you can add a patch to your denim.

Step 1:

Get a high quality needle and thread. You should ideally use a sashiko needle and thread it with sashiko fiber. When choosing the thread, make sure that it is either the color of the denim or it matches the color of the external patch. If the patch has multiple colors, then you should match the thread to the color at the border of the patch.

If you cannot find a thread that has a similar color as the patch or the denim, then you could choose a close darker shade.

You could also choose a lighter thread, but that depends on the results you expect. Do you want the thread to be easily noticeable, or would you like to blend it into the fabric as much as possible?

Step 2:

Position the patch in the way you prefer.

PRO TIP: Try out different angles and positions to find out what suits you best. You might have an idea of how to place the patch, but it does not hurt to experiment a little. Who knows? You might just discover a better alternative.

Step 3:

Use pins to secure the patch in place. If you like, you could also try out the denim and see how the patch looks on you. Of course, you have to be careful of the pins. Don't poke yourself for a simple trial!

Step 4:

Using a chalk or a dry soap, start adding lines to the fabric. The lines should resemble the same shape as the fabric, as close to its edges as possible. If possible, keep the line uninterrupted and continue drawing until you reach back to the point you started from.

Step 5:

Take out your needle and as usual, poke the

patch from the inner side of the denim. If your patch has corners, then it is better to start at one of the corners. However, if your patch is circular or does not have a corner, then you can start anywhere you like.

Step 6:

Use the lines to guide your stitches. For the patch, we shall go ahead and use a regular running stitch that we are now pretty good at using. You can use the quarter inch rule here as well with the stitches and the gaps.

Step 7:

If you run out of thread, simply use the techniques I had recommended in the previous chapters. However, for this purpose, I would simply recommend you measure 25 inches on the thread and begin using it for the stitch. Typically, most patches would not require you to use more than 25 inches. However, should you find yourself running out of thread, simply knot at a specific point and get the spool of thread to add more to the needle. Continue from where you left off by measure a quarter inch gap. Piece the material from the inner side of the material at the quarter inch mark.

Step 8:

Work your way around the fabric until you reach back to the beginning of your stitch. At this point, you could start threading in the opposite direction. This will allow you to close off the gaps that were originally there. This is not necessary and is entirely up to the result you are trying to achieve in your sewing. If you would like to find out how to close gaps, look at the chapter for Kantha to know more. When you reach the end, knot your thread.

Step 9:

Using your scissors, cut off any loose threads that you notice.

PRO TIP:

You know by now that you can get cotton from any old material or clothing. One of the ways to get fabric out of a material is by first measuring the area on which you would like to place the patch. Then, trace that area on another material. Cut out the fabric that meets your measurements and use that to sew it into your denim.

You can use multiple colors as well. For adding different colors, do refer to the boro tutorial mentioned above. It will give you a few ways in which you can use different colored fabrics.

Once you have finished your work, make sure you iron the fabric again. I would also recommend frequently ironing when you work to keep the fabric straight.

You can use the above technique to not only repair denim, but also add a bit of color and style. Try out different colors and shades until you find the one that is suitable for you. After that, it is just a matter of following the above instructions.

Chapter 6 - Yoeki: The Solution

When you are working with stitches, you often come across many questions that leave you befuddled. Each person's experience with sewing is unique. Some grasp concepts easily, but others take a while to master the process. This is in no way a reflection of the skills and abilities of the individual. Rather, it is how the individual prefers to learn.

I believe that everyone learns in their own way and at their own pace. This might be the case with you. Do not be deterred by the fact that others have learnt a skill quicker. The most important thing for you to remember is that you should revel in the learning process.

There is no competition. So take your time to master the techniques.

But in order to answer some of the questions that beginners might have, I have created a handy FAQ section right here. While the section does not involve a comprehensive list of questions, I based this on some of the most common questions I get asked about sewing.

Should you put the patch inside or outside the hole?

There are many reasons that can justify both options. Whether you would like to sew on the inside or on the outside entirely depends on what you aim to achieve and the type of patch you are working with.

Let us examine the result you would like to see on the denim.

If you plan to stitch a patch on the inside, then you get a subtle look. Something that is not outwardly presentable but still adds a sense of diversity to your denim. In other words, you can make your denim look stylish without having to display the style on the outside.

When you add a patch on the outside, then you are showing a bold look. You are showing off a bit of your personality in a very visible manner.

That being said, one of the main reasons that people should consider whether or not they should use a stitch on the inside or the outside is by examining the type of patch that they are working with.

If you are using a patch that has no designs and simply has a plain color, then you could place the patch on the inside of the denim. This serves two purposes.

- Placing a patch on the inside looks more aesthetically presentable than using the patch on the outside. You can, of course, experiment with different colors to find the one that fits your needs. But ideally, you should use the patch on the inside. Plus, revealing the tear while showing a material underneath it is quite a stylish addition.

- It is much more convenient to work from the inside. This is because you are typically piercing the patch from the inside. You can keep the outside for making markings for you to follow when sewing.

Again, it is also based on your decision. If you prefer to block the tear entirely, then you can choose to keep the patch on the outside.

On the other hand, if you have a patch that has some sort of print, text, image, or other design, then you should ideally use the patch on the outside. This is to ensure that the graphic is not blocked from view. In some cases, the graphic could be small enough for people to see through the tear in the denim. In such cases, you could use the patch on the inside with the graphic or pattern showing out.

There is no rule set in stone when you are working with patches. What you create is entirely up to you. As I had mentioned before, try and have fun with your creations and experiment with different styles. The best way to find out if the patch goes on the inside or on the outside is for you to test it out against the denim. If you are comfortable with the patch on the inside, then that is what you should choose. If you find out that the patch is meant to be outside, then you have your answer!

Should you make the patch bigger than the hole?

The simple answer to this question is yes. You should ideally look to make the patch bigger than the hole. This becomes important when you are working on the patch from the inside. You do not want to run out of patch when you are using a particular method of sewing. Additionally, you might decide to create a complex pattern on your denim. You might want the pattern to be seen clearly. With a larger patch on the inside, you have a bigger canvas for your sewing art!

Another factor to consider is that with a bigger patch, you can attach it to the denim more firmly. You can add more stitches and cross-stitches. to ensure that you have the fabric sewn properly into the denim.

On the other hand, if you are working on the patch from the outside, then you could use a patch that is almost the same size as the hole. This makes for an interesting effect. With the number of options available to you, you can experiment with the fabric to see what fits your needs.

I had provided this recommendation for the previous question, and it holds true for this one as well; try out the patch against the denim to see how it looks. If you are satisfied with the presentation, you can make up your mind after that.

Should you make extra stitches around the repair area?

When you are working with tears, gaps, and holes, one of the questions that you might find yourself frequently asking is whether or not you should add in extra stitches to your patch. For the previous question, I had mentioned how, by using an extra area of fabric, you can ensure that you sew the fabric properly into the denim.

But is that the only reason for considering

whether or not you would like to add extra stitches?

The entire act of creating stitches is an art in itself. You are using a simple – or complex – design and basically using it on your clothes (in this case, your denim). With that process alone, you are adding more designs and style to your denim than it had before. Would you like to show more of your stitches? Do you want to try adding different and more unique stitches around the repair area? Do you have a particular design in mind for the stitches that might require extra space?

By using just the running stitch technique, you can create many unique patterns on your denim. Some of these patterns do not require a lot of space, and you can sew them into the fabric you are using. Others might require more space, depending on the complexity and the number of lines you would like to use for the pattern.

Think about what you are going to sew and how you would like to accomplish it. Once you have figured out a rough idea for your stitches, you can choose how much area you would like to use.

Another thing to note at this point is that you do

not have to use extra space immediately. What I mean by this is that you might first use fewer lines, avoiding the use of extra stitches. If you change your mind later, you can always come back to your work and add more lines, depending on the pattern.

How to reinforce the inner thigh of your jeans?

Rips in the thighs of jeans are a potential threat to anyone who has thighs.

That's everyone.

However, some people experience this issue more than others.

The best way to deal with this problem is to reinforce your jeans from the inside. It is quite tempting simply to discard your jeans for a pair of new ones. You could always buy yourself new jeans. After all, a rip on the knee or almost anywhere else on the jeans does not look so bad, but one on your inner thigh might just be slightly embarrassing.

Thankfully, there is a simple way to reinforce your jeans so that you can prevent such rips and tears from occurring.

Before we start, we have to get the jeans ready

for sewing. Let us start with that.

Step 1:

Make sure you wash the jeans before you sew them. Ideally, you should turn the jeans inside out and let them have a proper wash.

Step 2:

Once they are dry, iron them while still keeping them inside out to remove any folds or creases on the jeans.

You are now ready to stitch on your jeans.

Make sure you have all your materials ready. You will need the materials mentioned in Chapter 1 for the most part. For the patch, you do not have to worry about choosing a specific color. If you can find other, similar jeans in your home, then cut out a small patch from those jeans. Regarding the measurements of the patch, I would recommend getting one that is 5 inches by 5 inches.

PRO TIP: If you would like to strengthen the reinforcement, then you can take two patches, both of which are 5 inches by 5 inches, and place them together.

If you would like to see how the size fits on your

jeans, then simply take a chalk, measure 5 inches by 5 inches, and draw the shape on your jeans. See if the size is ideal for you. If you prefer a bigger size, then draw that shape on your jeans and check if it satisfies your preference.

Once you have confirmed the size, you can then go about getting the patch from another pair of jeans. If you do not have jeans, you can also use cotton from any piece of clothing you have in your house (preferably one no one is using)!

Now you are ready to start stitching the patch into the inner thigh.

Step 1:

Now that your pants are inside out, you need to place an object (preferably a small book or a box) on the other side of the surface on which you are going to perform the stitching. This is to ensure that when you use your pins, you do not accidentally pin the legs of your jeans shut.

Step 2:

Since you are only reinforcing your jeans, find a thread color that has a darker shade than the jeans. This will help you hide it well. The best kind of thread is one that matches the color of the jeans. Such a thread would completely blend into the jeans.

Step 3:

Now place your patch where you would like it to be. Use pins to secure the patch to the jeans.

PRO TIP:

If you like, you can use the tip above where you can draw the outline of the patch on your jeans to see exactly where you would like the patch to be. Once you have the outline, you can place your patch on it.

Step 4:

Thread your needle. You can use the sashiko needle and thread for this stitching, or you could use any other needle and thread, the choice is yours.

Since the pattern of your stitching won't be visible to anyone, you do not need to draw lines to create a stitch pattern. However, you can use it to make sure you are stitching in a particular direction and don't suddenly find yourself stitching outside the patch area.

Step 5:

As always, run your needle from the inner side

of the jeans. This means that you will pierce from the side that is facing you. Typically, I would say that you should start piercing from the inner side, by which the needle would pierce out. This time, the needle will pierce in. The reason we are doing this is because once we complete the stitch, we will be tying the knot on the inside of the jeans, which is the side you are currently looking at. If the jeans were the right side out, then you would be piercing from the inside.

Step 6:

Use a running stitch method and continue stitching all the way around until you reach back to the starting point.

Step 7:

Upon reaching the starting point, create a knot to secure the patch to the jeans. The knot should be visible to you (unlike the previous cases where the knot was on the other side of the material). When you turn the jeans around, you will notice that the knot itself is not visible.

Step 8:

Now you are ready to wear your jeans. If you would like to perform the same technique on the inner thigh of the other leg, then you simply have to follow the same steps mentioned here.

You have now successfully reinforced your jeans!

10 Jean Repair Hacks

I have been placing some pro tips for you all throughout this book. However, I thought I would compile all the important hacks that I think you will find useful into one spot. Here are 10 jean repair hacks that you should know about.

- The first hack I would give you is more of advice; always fix the holes in your jeans rather than throwing them away.

- If you feel like your zipper is damaged beyond repair, then all you need to do is use a keyring to create a loop around your zipper and your jeans button.

- To add a splash of color, find a fabric or fabrics with floral prints and then sew them to your jeans.

- You do not have to stick to one layer for any repair; you can use up to three layers!

- Do not buy separate denim cutoffs – you can make them in your home using just your scissors.

- If you have a piece of gum stuck to your jeans, simply place a cube of ice on it for a while, and then remove it easily!

- When your jeans are loose at the waist, simply use an elastic band on the back of the jeans (where you find the loops) and stitch it to the pants.

- If your jeans button falls off, then stitch a piece of fabric behind the buttonhole and run the button and the snap through the fabric.

- To keep your jeans from shrinking in the wash, wash them using cold water, heat them for about ten minutes, and then air dry them if they are still damp.

- If you find your jeans decoloring, then simply place the jeans in a solution of water and vinegar for a while before sending them to the wash!

Leave A Review?

Throughout the process of writing this book, I have tried to put down as much value and knowledge for the reader as possible. Some things I knew and practice, some others I spent time to research. I hope you found this book to be of benefit to you!

If you liked the book, would you consider leaving a **quick review** for it? It would really help my book, and I would be grateful to you for letting other people know that you like it.

Ketsuron: The Conclusion

Fashion is a constantly evolving culture. It produces new designs, ideas, and products year after year. And every time a new statement is made, new clothing and apparels become the trend. However, fashion is also an industry that is capable of causing wastage in the form of discarded textiles and other materials.

To avoid such wastage and help make the industry sustainable, we can turn to the very source that creates the clothing and apparel: sewing. Using techniques like "minimal seam construction," which reduces the number of seams sewn into clothing, fashion can save materials and reduce waste. By reducing waste, fashion can contribute towards sustainability and help protect the environment.

But sewing does not just help the fashion industry. It helps people, too.

I have known people who claim that sewing is therapeutic. In fact, it is not just the people I know, but a majority of the public that has begun to work with the sewing craft. One of the things that you might hear quite often is that the process has been shown to have some remarkable effects on managing stress.

Mental effects notwithstanding, everyone has a different reason for working with hand sewing. Some have chosen to hone their skills so that they may eventually start a business out of it. Some prefer to use sewing as a form of a hobby. Still others aim to satiate their curiosity.

Whatever your reasons for entering the sewing world are, remember that like all other forms of art, it requires practice to become a master. But with sewing, the satisfaction, enjoyment, and fulfillment do not lie in the fact that you are eventually going to be really good at the craft. Rather, it lies in the very act of practicing hand sewing.

My biggest advice would be this: take your time with each technique. When you have gained a fair amount of confidence with a technique, then try a different pattern and see how well you do. The whole idea behind sewing is to use your creativity to come up with interesting designs. After all, there are those who have stitched even things like animal patterns into fabrics!

You could also use numerous sewing practice kits that are specifically made for you to try out patterns, techniques, and even different types of tools.

With that, I hope you enjoy hand sewing.

Tanoshinde!

www.ingramcontent.com/pod-product-compliance
Lightning Source LLC
Chambersburg PA
CBHW020130130526
44591CB00032B/585